STOUGHTON PUBLIC L[...]  P9-DMD-500
304 S. FOURTH ST.
STOUGHTON, WI 53589

Presented to

The Stoughton
Public Library

In Memory of

Cal & Ellie

Koberstein

From "Friends & Family"
2015

IT'S A FACT! Real-Life Reads

The Life of a
GLADIATOR

by Ruth Owen

Series consultant:

Suzy Gazlay, MA
Recipient, Presidential Award for Excellence in Science Teaching

Ruby Tuesday Books

Published in 2015 by Ruby Tuesday Books Ltd.

Copyright © 2015 Ruby Tuesday Books Ltd.

All rights reserved. No part of this publication may be reproduced in whole or in part, stored in any retrieval system, or transmitted in any form or by any means, electronic, mechanical, photocopying, recording, or otherwise, without written permission from the publisher.

Editor: Mark J. Sachner
Designer: Emma Randall
Production: John Lingham

Photo Credits:
Alamy: 8, 12, 26; Corbis: 9, 24; Cosmographics: 6; Getty Images: 15; Public Domain: 10–11, 16, 20, 25, 27; Shutterstock: Cover, 4–5, 7, 13, 14 (Nito), 17, 18–19 (Juan G. Aunion), 19 (top), 21, 22, 23 (Pixelite), 29 (top: Juan G. Aunion), 29 (center), 29 (bottom: Nito), 31.

Library of Congress Control Number: 2014920845

ISBN 978-1-909673-96-0

Printed and published in the United States of America

For further information including rights and permissions requests, please contact our Customer Service Department at 877-337-8577.

Contents

A Deadly Sport

In Roman times, cheering crowds packed large stadiums to watch their favorite sport.

In the **arena**, pairs of super fit, highly skilled contestants went head to head. A contest might last for 30 minutes, or it might all be over in 60 seconds. For the winner, there were prizes and the cheers of adoring fans. For the loser, it might mean a final journey through the "gate of the dead."

The word "gladiator" means "a man of the sword." It comes from the word *gladius*, which is the **Latin** word for "sword."

It was brutal. It was bloody. And the ancient Romans couldn't get enough.

This was history's most deadly sport—the gladiator games.

Gladiator Games

Ancient Rome was a **civilization** that existed in present-day Italy.

Its citizens loved to watch gladiators. The first fights between Roman gladiators took place at funerals. The fights were a way to honor the dead.

A Map of the Roman Empire in the Year 180

The most important place in the Roman world was the great city of Rome. It was founded in the year 753 BC.

N
W E
S

EUROPE

Italy

Black Sea

Rome

Mediterranean Sea

MIDDLE EAST

AFRICA

The powerful Roman army invaded parts of Europe, the Middle East, and North Africa. All these conquered lands (shown in orange on the map) became part of the **Roman Empire.**

In time, the **emperor** and other important Romans began to organize gladiator games. Roman leaders wanted to be popular with the people they ruled. So they arranged exciting and bloody events that rich and poor Romans could enjoy. Gladiator games were held in stadiums called **amphitheaters**.

In the year 107, Emperor Trajan organized gladiator games in Rome. They lasted for 123 days. More than 5,000 pairs of gladiators fought each other at this event.

The Romans built amphitheaters across the Roman Empire. This is the ruin of an amphitheater in Tunisia in North Africa. It was built 1,800 years ago.

A Deadly Choice

In Roman times, thousands of gladiators were killed. So why would anyone become a gladiator? Many people simply had no choice.

When the Roman army invaded another country, the soldiers took prisoners. Many of these prisoners were forced to become gladiators.

This Roman sculpture shows two female gladiators. Most gladiators were men, but some women also appeared in gladiator games.

The Romans had many ways to **execute** criminals. Some were **crucified** or killed with a sword. They might also be torn apart by wild animals, as shown in this Roman **mosaic**.

A criminal who committed a serious crime, such as murder, was sentenced to death. Instead of execution, however, he might be given the choice of becoming a gladiator. Then he could escape death—at least for a short while!

Not all gladiators were forced to fight. Some young men were very poor or in debt. They became gladiators to win prize money. Others signed up because the danger and excitement of a gladiator's life was too much to resist.

Gladiator School

Once a man became a gladiator, he was sent to a *ludus*, or gladiator school.

The gladiator became the property of a manager called a *lanista*. The lanista owned all the gladiators in his school. He then made money by hiring them out to the organizers of gladiator games.

Many different people worked at a ludus. A *medicus*, or doctor, took care of the gladiators if they became sick or injured. There was a repair man to fix the fighters' armor and weapons. There was even a costumes man. He made sure the gladiators looked as good as possible in the arena!

Every new gladiator had to swear an **oath**. This showed he accepted his possible doom. A gladiator agreed:

To be burned, flogged, beaten, or slain by cold steel, as my owner should order.

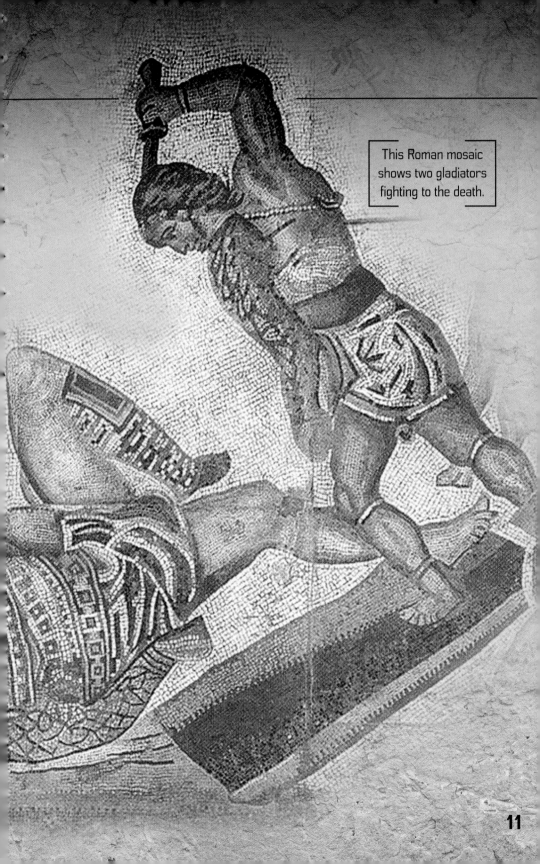

This Roman mosaic shows two gladiators fighting to the death.

Learning to Fight

Once a new gladiator swore the oath, he became a *tiro*, or trainee gladiator.

A trainee practiced fighting against a tall wooden pole called a *palus*. For hour after hour, he hacked at the palus with a wooden sword. The weapons a gladiator used for training were heavier than the real thing. This built up his strength and **stamina**.

These are the ruins of the gladiator training school in the Roman city of Pompeii, in Italy.

At a ludus, all the real weapons were kept locked away. This stopped the men who were prisoners or criminals from stealing them and starting trouble!

A trainee learned how to block blows to protect his own body. He also learned how to do maximum damage to his opponent's body. A cut across a man's stomach could release his intestines onto the sand. A slash across the back of an opponent's knees would make it impossible for him to stand.

Gladiators were trained by a man called a *doctor*. The trainer was usually an ex-gladiator who had survived many fights.

Gladiator in Training

For hour after hour, day after day, month after month, a new gladiator trained. Finally, the lanista decided what kind of gladiator the trainee would become.

A big man would be selected to join the *scutarii*, or "shield carriers." This group included the *provocators*, the *murmillos*, and the *secutors*. These gladiators fought with swords and carried large, heavy shields.

The "small shield fighters" were the *hoplomachi* and the *Thracians*. These gladiators were lighter, fast-moving men. They fought with swords, daggers, and small shields.

These actors are showing how gladiators fought with large shields.

Provocator means "the challenger."

Murmillo means "the fish man."

Secutor means "the chaser."

Hoplomachus means "Hoplite fighter." These gladiators were armed like Greek Hoplite soldiers.

A *Thracian* was a gladiator armed like a warrior from the ancient people called Thracians.

A Thracian gladiator's helmet

All these gladiators wore heavy helmets, padded arm guards, and metal leg guards called greaves. A gladiator's helmet made him seem less human. This made it easier for another fighter to kill him!

The Net Man

There was one type of gladiator who wore no helmet. He also did not carry a shield. This was the fast-moving "net man," or *retiarius*.

A retiarius was armed with a dagger and a long, fork-like trident. He also carried a circular net that was about 9 feet (3 m) wide.

Net

This sculpture shows a secutor fighting a retiarius. A secutor's egg-shaped helmet had tiny eye holes. This made it difficult for him to keep track of the retiarius and his net.

IMPROBVM

A retiarius usually fought a secutor. The net man had to be fast on his feet to dodge his opponent's sword. The retiarius stabbed at the secutor with his trident. He swept his net near the secutor's feet to try to trip him. He also threw the net and tried to capture his opponent. Once the secutor was tangled in the net, he could not escape or fight back.

Secutor

Retiarius

Trident

Wide belt to protect the stomach

Life Behind the Scenes

At night, the men in a ludus were locked in small cells. By day, they trained until they were exhausted.

There was one good thing about being a gladiator—plenty to eat! Gladiators ate very little meat, but lots of fruit and vegetables. They also ate a porridge-like food made of barley and beans.

The gladiators' diet helped them build up muscles and pack on fat. A layer of fat helped protect a man's insides. If the fat was slashed by a sword, it bled a lot. This pleased the crowd, who loved to see lots of blood. The gladiator could still fight on, though, and look extra brave.

Gladiators needed calcium to make their bones strong. To get calcium, they drank a disgusting mixture. It contained ash from burned bones and wood.

Gladiators lived and trained together. Each man knew that one day in the arena, he might have to kill a friend.

19

Ready for Action

Gladiators practiced their moves over and over. Eventually, each man became an automatic fighting machine!

A gladiator might take part in gladiator games just three times a year. The rest of the time he trained for hours each day.

Romans loved to talk about gladiator fights. Just like today's sports stars, a winning gladiator could become famous. His fans would cheer for him in the arena. They would discuss his strength, stamina, skills, and bravery.

In Roman society, however, gladiators were thought of as lowly. A gladiator might be a hero in the arena. In everyday life, however, he was an *infamis*, or low life. No number of victories could ever change that.

Items decorated with gladiators were popular in Roman times. This flask shows a fight between a Murmillo and a Thracian.

Gladiators were super fit. Many gladiators probably looked like modern-day body builders.

Just like today's movie stars and pop stars, gladiators used stage names. This helped to hide their true identities.

Welcome to the Colosseum

A gladiator who trained in Rome would fight in the greatest amphitheater of all—the Colosseum.

This huge building covers as much ground as five football fields. It could seat more than 50,000 spectators. Every spectator was given a ticket that showed him or her where to sit. The emperor gave free tickets to the poor to keep them happy.

The crowd sat on stone seats. They bought snacks and cups of wine from food sellers. Sometimes, officials threw small wooden balls into the crowd. Each one showed a prize that could be claimed by the person who caught the ball. A spectator might win some food, a vase, a horse, or even some gold.

The Colosseum was as tall as a 14-story building. People can still visit the ruins of the Colosseum today.

The emperor and other important Romans sat closest to the arena.
Women were seated in the highest seats, farthest from the action.

In Roman times, the arena
had a wooden floor. It was
covered with sand to soak
up the blood.

The Colosseum had many wide entrances to let spectators in
and out. The entrances were called *vomitoria*.

A Day at the Games

For Romans, a day at the Colosseum was a bloody and violent treat.

The first events of the day were animal fights. The Romans captured wild animals from all over the empire. The hungry animals were set loose in the arena to attack and kill each other. Next, highly trained animal fighters hunted and fought with the terrified creatures.

A day at the games began with a huge parade around the arena.

At lunchtime, the executions began. As the crowd cheered, criminals were torn apart by wild animals. The executions showed Romans what could happen if they broke the law. To cover the smell of blood, perfumed water was sprayed into the crowd.

Finally, it was time for the main event—the gladiators!

Elephants, rhinos, hippos, lions, tigers, leopards, and even crocodiles were brought to the Colosseum. Men called *bestiarii* were trained to fight the animals.

A Fight to the Death

By the afternoon, the crowd in the Colosseum was in a frenzy of excitement.

Two by two, pairs of gladiators entered the arena to fight. The gladiators stabbed at each other. They blocked. They counter-stabbed. Finally, badly injured, one man would fall to the ground. This was the moment the crowd had waited for. Should the losing fighter live or die? If the man had fought well, the crowd might shout for mercy. If not, they screamed for his death.

The emperor listened to his people, and then made his decision. Many times, the decision was death. Then, the winning gladiator would deal a final killer blow to his opponent.

A summa rudis

A referee called a *summa rudis* watched over the fight. Once a gladiator was too injured to continue, the referee stopped the fight.

The emperor used his thumb to show that a losing gladiator should die. Historians believe it made no difference whether he gave a thumbs up or a thumbs down. It always meant the same thing—death!

Victory, Mercy, or Death

As the crowd cheered, a winning gladiator received his prizes.

He was awarded a branch from a palm tree. He might also win some prize money.

A gladiator who had escaped death was carried from the arena by slaves. In the *saniarum*, or hospital, his injuries were treated. He had survived to fight another day. A gladiator who had been killed was carried from the arena through the "gate of the dead." To make certain he was really dead, his throat was cut.

Some gladiators lived long enough to receive the *rudis*, or wooden sword. This meant they could retire. Some men then became trainers. Others became bodyguards to wealthy Romans.

Over hundreds of years, however, many thousands of gladiators were killed. Only a lucky few survived their careers in history's deadliest sport.

Actors show a summa rudis checking an injured gladiator. The winner waits to receive his prizes.

Glossary

amphitheater (AM-fi-thee-tur)
A circular or oval-shaped building used for sports contests, plays, and other events. The building had layers of seats rising up from an arena.

arena (uh-REE-nuh)
An area surrounded by seats where sports contests or other events take place. The word "arena" comes from the Latin word *harena*, which means "sand."

civilization (civ-il-uh-ZAY-shuhn)
A large group of people from a particular area that share the same history, culture, and way of life.

crucified (KROO-si-fide)
Executed by being tied or nailed to a large wooden cross and left to die.

emperor (EM-pur-ur)
The leader of an empire.

execute (EKS-uh-kyoot)
Put a person to death, usually as a punishment for a very serious crime.

Latin (LAT-uhn)
An ancient language that was spoken by Roman people and many people throughout the Roman Empire.

mosaic (mo-ZAY-ik)
A picture created from thousands of tiny pieces of stone, tile, or glass. The Romans decorated walls and floors with mosaics.

oath (OHTH)
A promise that is often made in front of witnesses.

Roman Empire (ROH-muhn EM-pire)
The parts of the world that were conquered and ruled over by the Romans. The empire included Italy and parts of Europe, North Africa, and the Middle East.

stamina (STAM-uh-nuh)
The ability to carry out a physical activity over a long period of time.

Index

Read More

Murrell, Deborah. *Gladiator (QEB Warriors)*. Mankato, MN: Black Rabbit Books (2009).

Phillips, Dee. *Gladiator: The Story of a Fighter (Yesterday's Voices)*. Costa Mesa, CA: Saddleback Educational Publishing (2014).

Learn More Online

To learn more about gladiators, go to
www.rubytuesdaybooks.com/gladiator